Ladies Love Yourselves First, That's Happiness
Workbook & Journal

Ladies Love Yourselves First, That's Happiness Workbook & Journal

Cadori

All Rights Reserved. No portion of this book may be reproduced, stored in a retrieval system, or transmitted in any form or by any means-electronic, mechanical, photocopy, recording, scanning, or other- except for brief quotation in critical reviews or articles, without the prior permission of the publisher.

Published by Game Changer Publishing

ISBN 978-1-7371654-2-2

Game Changer PUBLISHING

www.PublishABestSellingBook.com

FREE BONUS GIFTS

Just to say thanks for purchasing my journal, I would like to give you
a few free bonus gifts, no strings attached!

To Download Now, Visit:
www.CadoriTheAuthor.com/CM/FreeGiftJournal

Ladies Love Yourselves First, That's Happiness
Workbook & Journal

Cadori

Game Changer PUBLISHING

www.PublishABestSellingBook.com

Table of Contents

Chapter 1 - Mistakes 1

Chapter 2 - Childhood Trauma 3

Chapter 3 - Settling For The Bottom 9

Chapter 4 - Inner Circle and Accountability 13

Chapter 5 - There Are No Perfect People 17

Chapter 6 - Red Flags 21

Chapter 7 - Me Time & Self Reflection 25

Chapter 8 - Choose To Be Happy & Protect Your Peace 29

Chapter 9 - Distance Yourself From Negative People 33

Chapter 10 - Manifest What You Want 37

Chapter 11 - Woman Warrior 41

Chapter 12 - Stand In Your Power & Never Give Up 43

CHAPTER 1
Mistakes

1 List at least one costly mistake(s) that you made in life and the lesson(s) you learned from it.
_____
_____
_____
_____
_____
_____

2 What steps can you take to avoid making this same mistake(s) again?
_____
_____
_____
_____
_____
_____

3 If you had to teach someone you love how to avoid this mistake(s) what would you tell them?
_____
_____
_____
_____
_____
_____

NOTES

CHAPTER 2
Childhood Trauma

1 Write down your childhood trauma(s).

_____
_____
_____
_____
_____
_____

2 How does that childhood trauma(s) make you feel right now?

_____
_____
_____
_____
_____
_____

3 Why do you think that childhood trauma(s) still affects you in this way?

_____
_____
_____
_____
_____
_____

4 If you could view this childhood trauma(s) in a more positive way would you?

_____
_____
_____
_____
_____
_____
_____

5 What's stopping you from viewing this childhood trauma in a positive way?

_____
_____
_____
_____
_____
_____
_____

6 If you viewed it as a testimony to help someone else would that make a difference in how you viewed it?

_____
_____
_____
_____
_____
_____
_____

7 If you looked at yourself as a Survivor and as someone who is Strong because you are still alive and capable of being anything that you want to be if you choose to decide to use your brain to view this trauma differently, think about the positive shift that would instantly take place in your life.

_____
_____
_____
_____
_____
_____
_____

8 List one thing you have always wanted to do but didn't do because this childhood trauma(s) has been holding you back your entire life?

_____
_____
_____
_____
_____
_____
_____

9 Now write out some steps you can take to make that thing a reality.

_____
_____
_____
_____
_____
_____
_____

10 Have you thought about seeking a professional mental health therapist?

_____
_____
_____
_____
_____
_____

Even if you've tried one before and it didn't work out you can always try others because therapists are people too, meaning there are some that just don't connect with you but others would connect. You never know until you keep trying and don't give up on yourself. You have one beautiful precious life and whatever changes it takes for you to feel happy and live the rest of your life fulfilling the dreams that you want to fulfill then those changes are well worth it because YOU are worth it!

NOTES

CHAPTER 3

Settling For The Bottom

1 List one thing that you know that you have settled for.
_____
_____
_____
_____
_____
_____

2 Why did you settle for this instead of pushing for what you truly deserve?
_____
_____
_____
_____
_____
_____

3 If you could change what you settled for today would you change it?
_____
_____
_____
_____
_____
_____

4 If the answer is "NO" then why wouldn't you change it?

_____
_____
_____
_____
_____
_____
_____
_____
_____

5 If the answer is "YES" let's start by writing down at least one thing that you can do to change the behavior that caused you to settle in the first place, which is operating out of a "Lack Of" mindset. (On this question think about how you were raised and what impact did your surroundings have on you and your mindset of just settling.)

_____
_____
_____
_____
_____
_____
_____
_____

6 Now write down something(s) you can do everyday to help change your mindset to become an "Abundance" mindset as opposed to a "Lack Of" mindset. (It could be something as simple as reading positive affirmations everyday and posting them on your bathroom mirror, in your bedroom, living room, kitchen, your car and at your workstation and on your cell phone so you can always see positivity. It really does change your mindset!

_____
_____
_____
_____
_____
_____
_____
_____
_____
_____

NOTES

CHAPTER 4

Inner Circle and Accountability

1 List the 5 closest people to you that you frequently talk to almost daily?

_____
_____
_____
_____
_____
_____
_____
_____
_____

2 Next to each person's name I want you to be completely honest with yourself and write down if the person is bringing positivity into your life by encouraging you to excel in life or is the person bringing negativity into your life or just simply existing in life without any drive or motivation.

_____
_____
_____
_____
_____
_____
_____

Because that person is actually helping to hold you back in life to be completely honest with you. People are either helping you to excel in life or helping to keep you right where you are.

_____
_____
_____
_____
_____
_____

So next to each name write down what each person in your inner circle is doing in your life.

_____
_____
_____
_____
_____
_____

3 This next step is critical. Decide who is going to be moved out of your inner circle in order for you to move forward in life and excel by living your dreams and fulfilling your purpose in life. Because everyone CANNOT go with you. You cannot reach your highest level with negative or stagnant people in your inner circle, period.

_____
_____
_____
_____
_____

NOTES

CHAPTER 5
There Are No Perfect People

1 Who do you think has a perfect life? (It can be someone you know personally or a celebrity, but list someone.)

___

2 Why do you think their life is perfect? (Is it their money or status or something else?)

___

3 If you take away their money or status or whatever they have that you think makes them perfect, how would you view them now?

_____
_____
_____
_____
_____
_____
_____

Truth is, regardless of whether a person has money, or status or whatever else we may think gives them a pass in life to appear perfect, they are still human. The thing that we all have to be willing to accept is this, No One Is Perfect! No One! Some of the same problems and issues in life that you deal with, they deal with. They have health issues, they experience loss of a loved one just like everyone else, they have relationship problems, if they get cut they will bleed just like you will bleed if you get cut, they have money problems just on a larger scale, they are affected by storms and bad weather, they are also living in the same world as everyone else trying to survive the Pandemic! I challenge You to start thinking that Everyone has problems and No One is Perfect.

4 Write This Down and Say it Out Loud….."There Are No Perfect People"

_____
_____
_____
_____
_____
_____
_____

NOTES

CHAPTER 6
Red Flags

1 List a Red Flag that you noticed in a relationship but didn't pay it no mind?

_____
_____
_____
_____
_____
_____

2 What was the negative effect of not paying attention to that Red Flag?

_____
_____
_____
_____
_____
_____

3 How do you handle Red Flags when you notice them in a relationship now?

_____
_____
_____
_____
_____
_____

4 What would you teach someone you loved about Red Flags?

_____
_____
_____
_____
_____

5 If you have not changed your behavior when noticing a Red Flag in a relationship, ask yourself, why not?

_____
_____
_____
_____
_____

NOTES

CHAPTER 7

Me Time & Self Reflection

1 Do you ever spend alone time with yourself telling yourself positive things about yourself?

_____
_____
_____
_____
_____
_____
_____

2 If not, why not?

_____
_____
_____
_____
_____
_____
_____

3 List one thing you love about yourself?

_____
_____
_____
_____
_____
_____
_____

4 Do you frequently do self care and self love things for yourself at least on a weekly basis?

_____
_____
_____
_____
_____

5 If not, why not?

_____
_____
_____
_____
_____

It's important to know that every time we pour into other people cups and they don't pour back into our cups that our cups will become bone dry! It's our responsibility to hold ourselves accountable for our actions, And to hold others accountable for their actions as well. Think about that as you go about your day and as you decide who you want to pour into. Be intentional about your relationships with people and make sure that you are in mutually giving relationships otherwise you will set yourself up for unwanted stress and unhappiness.

NOTES

CHAPTER 8

Choose To Be Happy & Protect Your Peace

1 Did you know that happiness is a choice?

_____
_____
_____
_____
_____
_____

2 Did you know that you control the majority of your happiness?

_____
_____
_____
_____
_____

3 What are some things that you are doing right now to make yourself happy?

_____
_____
_____
_____
_____

4 Do you try to avoid negative conversations about other people or do you run to those conversations?

___

Because if you continue to listen to negativity all day long, you are feeding yourself unhappiness. We all have a choice on what we absorb both mentally and nutritiously.

5 Are you intentional about what you watch on social media and on TV?

___

We all like to watch an array of movies and tv shows and videos. But did you know if you consume more than 20 percent of negativity and drama in a day that you are telling your body that you like negativity and drama and you don't want peace. Because you are choosing to allow those things into your psyche.

6 Make a list of things you can do to protect your peace.

NOTES

CHAPTER 9
Distance Yourself From Negative People, Including Some Family Members

1 Are there negative people in your inner circle, your five close friends or family members?

_____
_____
_____
_____
_____
_____
_____
_____

2 Are you a supportive person or a non supportive person? If you are a non supportive person can you tell me why you are non supportive?

_____
_____
_____
_____
_____
_____
_____
_____

3 If you are a supportive person, do you get support equally given back to you from the people you support?

_____
_____
_____
_____
_____
_____
_____

4 If not, have you told them about how that makes you feel?

_____
_____
_____
_____
_____
_____
_____

If you haven't told them then you should tell them to give them a chance to correct the behavior. Once you tell them then it's on them to change it. If they don't change the behavior and start reciprocating the support then it's on you to stop supporting them. Because every time you pour into others and they don't reciprocate that same behavior towards you, then you will become drained inside and you question your self worth. We as humans crave love and affection and kindness and when we give those things and don't receive them back it has negative consequences on our psyche and our bodies. This is why it is so important to surround yourself with like minded people and it is our responsibility to hand pick the people who are in our inner circle and choose people who treat us like we treat them.

NOTES

CHAPTER 10
Manifest What You Want

1 List a few things that you desire? Do you truthfully believe that you can and should have these things 100%?

_____
_____
_____
_____
_____
_____
_____

2 What have you actively been doing to acquire these things other than talking?

_____
_____
_____
_____
_____

3 How frequently are you doing things to acquire these things?

_____
_____
_____
_____
_____

4 Are you talking to people who can help you acquire these things or are you talking to people who are non supportive?

_____
_____
_____
_____
_____
_____
_____
_____

Because if you are sharing your vision with people who are non supportive or negative then that's part of the reason why you don't have those things that you desire. Your dreams and visions should NOT be shared with anyone who is non-supportive or negative, and that includes family members! You will have to learn to move in silence and to protect your vision by not sharing it with everybody. Those people are putting negative energy towards your vision and that's definitely part of the reason it has not become a reality.

5 Write down your vision and be as detailed as possible.

_____
_____
_____
_____
_____
_____
_____

6 Write down the steps that you need to take to get there.

_____
_____
_____
_____
_____
_____
_____
_____
_____

Pray about it everyday and do something to work towards it everyday. That's manifesting it into your life. When things don't turn out the way you expect it to then do your research and try another approach. If you believe with everything in you that this dream or vision is yours then it is yours! It's already happened it just hasn't quite yet materialized before you but it's already done. So never ever give up on your dreams!

NOTES

CHAPTER 11

Woman Warrior

1 Do you believe that there is a Woman Warrior inside of you that is capable of doing and being anything that she wants to be?

_____
_____
_____
_____
_____
_____
_____
_____
_____

Then repeat after me….. " I AM A WOMAN WARRIOR"

NOTES

CHAPTER 12

Stand In Your Power & Never Give Up

1 Tell me who you are as a person? Are you kind or a giver or do you have something that helps others or are you an introvert or a quick tempered angry person or a judgmental person or a dramatic person? Whoever you are tell me.

_____

2 Now tell me are you happy being this person or do you want to change some things about yourself?

_____

3 Why do you want to change yourself? Is it because you truly want to be different or because other people want you to be different?

_____

_____

_____

_____

_____

_____

_____

4 Are you truly happy being you just the way you are right now?

_____

_____

_____

_____

_____

_____

_____

Because I'll tell you this. You are a Unique person, and unless you truly need to change something about yourself then don't change a thing.

Because No One is perfect and never will be perfect. So before you go changing yourself to please others, just make sure that you are making changes in your life for the better for You!

Because at the end of the day You live inside of your body and You have to be 100 % sure that You are happy with yourself everyday!

There's Only One YOU on the Planet! You are Powerful! Learn to Be Yourself Unapologetically and Learn to Love Yourself Unconditionally. ♥

NOTES

NOTES

NOTES

NOTES

NOTES

NOTES

NOTES

NOTES

NOTES

NOTES

NOTES

NOTES

NOTES

NOTES

NOTES

NOTES

NOTES

NOTES

NOTES

NOTES

NOTES

NOTES

NOTES

NOTES

NOTES

NOTES

NOTES

NOTES

NOTES

NOTES

NOTES

NOTES

NOTES

NOTES

NOTES

NOTES

NOTES

NOTES

NOTES

NOTES

NOTES

NOTES

NOTES

NOTES

NOTES

NOTES

FREE BONUS GIFTS

Just to say thanks for purchasing my journal, I would like to give you
a few free bonus gifts, no strings attached!

To Download Now, Visit:
www.CadoriTheAuthor.com/CM/FreeGiftJournal

I appreciate your interest in my book, and I value your feedback as it helps me improve future versions of this book. I would appreciate it if you could leave your invaluable review on Amazon.com with your feedback. Thank you!

Made in the USA
Columbia, SC
06 November 2024